Introduc

C000242058

The busy, friendly market town of Rha
the Cambrian Mountains. Well served
and cafés, the town lies within a sublime landscape w.....
and moorland from the basin of the Wye Valley. The high land to the west is
increasingly and happily being referred to by its ancient name, Elenydd, and
is one of the loneliest and wildest spaces south of the Scottish border.

The region's open landscape may appear to be in its wild state, but
man's impact upon it has been long term and draconian. Large areas would
have once been covered with dwarf oak woodlands, the delightful remnants of
which are encountered on some of the walks in this book, and the monuments
of early settlers still adorn the plateau, adding a powerful historical resonance
to our modern wanderings.

In subsequent millennia, mankind has continued to play a decisive role
in the development of the landscape, chiefly through sheep farming. The
Cistercian monks profitably managed sheepwalks in the medieval period,
and a section of their ancient road between the abbeys of Cwm Hir and Strata
Florida provides one of the most striking routes in this book.

Industry has long been a part of man's relationship with this land, and
the story of metal mining is etched into the hills. The mining industry was
in terminal decline by the late nineteenth century, when the Corporation of
Birmingham was beginning work on one of the defining features of the modern mid-Wales landscape, the Elan Valley dams. Construction stole away
thousands of acres of the Welsh countryside as well as several hundred liveli-
hoods, an evil not outweighed by the free access allowed to this new found
wilderness. Whatever the rights and wrongs of the past, the Gothic architecture of the dams and their attendant reservoirs add a powerful theme to walks
in the Elan Valley.

Man's relationship with these hills is not of course over. Having avoided
the worst of the conifer blight, the central Elenydd will not escape the visual
impact of wind turbines, which have been multiplying in recent years. Like
the mines, they form a provocative statement, and will doubtless exercise the
minds and consciences of many walkers.

Each walk has a detailed map and description which enables the route
to be followed without difficulty, but be aware that changes can occur at any
time, and the conditions of the paths can vary with the seasons and the weather (you can get a weather forecast on 09014 722064). Walking boots are recommended, along with appropriate clothing to protect against the elements.
The location of each walk is shown on the back cover and a summary of their
key features is also given. This includes an estimated walking time, but allow
extra time to enjoy the scenery. Please observe the country code.

Enjoy your walking!

THE WYE VALLEY (SOUTH)

DESCRIPTION A very pleasant and for the most part simple walk which explores the Wye Valley immediately to the south of Rhayader. There is a slight sting in the tail, which involves either fording the River Wye or re-tracing your steps. If you decide not to cross the Wye the walk is just over five miles in length, and just over three miles, if a crossing is successful. Assume that you will have to double back and allow two and a half hours.

START Rhayader Town Centre

I Head along the main street of Rhayader, with the Spar shop on the left, and leave town, crossing the bridge over the Wye. Turn left along a lane, which is signposted as the Wye Valley Walk, *and which forms part of the National Trail of that name.* Continue past the playing fields on your left, and the church of Sant Ffraid on your right, and climb gently away from the town. As you climb, the surrounding hills come into view. *The cairn of Gwastedyn Hill is clearly visible on the south-east horizon, as is the scar of the huge stone quarry at its foot.* About half a mile out of town the road takes a sharp turn to the left. Ignore this, and continue along the dusty track (clearly marked as the continuation of the Wye Valley Walk) which goes straight on. This drops gently towards the valley bottom until it brings you to an old railway line, behind which are some substantial farm buildings. Turn left before reaching the railway line and follow the bridleway (still marked as the Wye Valley Walk) past a well preserved set of traditional Radnorshire farm buildings, *which offer a pointed contrast to the much larger and far less aesthetic modern constructions below.* Ignore the temptation to follow the road under the dismantled rail bridge, and continue past a disused quarry (which seems to have found new purpose as a private rubbish dump) on the left. Then follow the Wye Valley Walk along a footpath which runs parallel to the disused railway, and then alongside a fine patch of mature woodland. All too quickly you will arrive at tarmac.

2 Turn left to start the homeward leg. Fortunately the road is but a very minor country lane, barely frequented by motorised traffic. In any case, it is soon left behind as the route turns right at the first opportunity, heading through a double gate which heads into a mature forestry plantation. Follow the unambiguously marked bridleway down through the forestry, which, although coniferous, gives delightful walking. *Buzzards circled above my head when I walked this stretch.* After half a mile of leisurely walking, the forest ends and the route passes through a gate into scrub land. Continue through the scrub on the still obvious path until it reaches the yard of Ddole Farm. As the farm is approached the first glimpses of the River Wye are gained, although the sewage works across the river do somewhat detract from its beauty at this particular point! Turn left out of the farm and then go right through a gate, along a signposted bridleway which takes you down to the banks of the Wye. *This section more than makes up for the recent intrusion of the sewage works, and allows intimate contact with this most beautiful of rivers.* A blissful quarter of a mile will bring you to an elbow in the river.

3 *At this point things become a little complicated.* The bridleway goes straight on through the river. *This may be feasible on a horse, but may only be attractive to a hard-core of walkers – and then only in the summer if the water level is very low!* Note that this should only be attempted in dry weather when the water is low. Any attempt to cross the river in anything other than very dry conditions would be dangerous and highly stupid. **We do not recommend this crossing.** If the bridge (which is tantalisingly shown on the 1:50,000 Ordnance Survey map) has not been re-instated, you will need to turn back and re-trace your steps along the Wye, back through Ddole farm, and along the woodland track. This is, however, no hardship, and

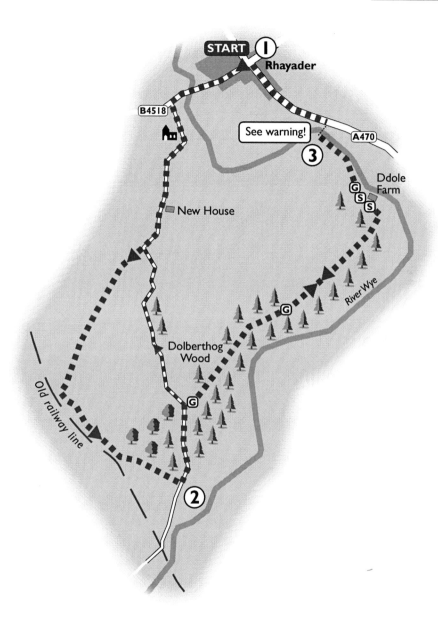

allows you to enjoy the Wye valley in the other direction. Once through the woodland, turn right at the minor tarmac road and follow it all the way back to Rhayader.

AROUND CASTLE HILL

DESCRIPTION A gentle and well waymarked lowland walk that explores the countryside to the east of Rhayader. It takes the soft dome of Castle Hill as its theme, circumnavigating it on public footpaths through fields and woodland. Lots of rickety stiles to climb.
START Gaufron Village.
DIRECTIONS Leave Rhayader on the A44. Gaufron is less than two miles outside Rhayader. Look at for some disused petrol pumps, but note that the chapel marked on the OS map has been demolished. There is space to park on the right hand side of the main road near the petrol pumps, and next to the memorial space on which the chapel once stood.

From Gaufron cross the main road to find a footpath, which goes down into a field and joins an obvious track. Follow this track. On the map a public right of way bears right through some marshy scrubland, but this is fenced off on the ground and the track seems to be an accepted and more practical diversion. Turn right when you reach a junction, which is at the foot of Castle Hill, and continue along the track. After passing through a series of gates you will arrive at the farm of Neauddllwyd. Abandon the track and walk directly to the right hand side of the farmhouse, to follow a footpath between two sheds that enters the field behind it. Cross a small enclosure, containing an abandoned car, and negotiate a stile near its top corner. Follow the waymarks across fields, climbing another stile, passing an antique abandoned tractor, and going through two more gates. *As you walk, the surroundings become ever more tranquil, as any noise from the main road in the valley behind you recedes into the far distance. Across the valley of the Dulas the hills above Nantmel enclose the view, as they work their way up into the extensive sweep of Camlo Hill.* Before long you will reach the farm of Great Castle.

2 Follow the public footpath through a small gate and around the back of the house to cross a stile onto a track. Follow this track until you arrive at Little Castle, which (except for the concrete block addition to its rear) is a good example of Radnorshire vernacular architecture. At Little Castle, in order to stay on the public footpath you will need to go to the right of the building and locate a gate beneath the main track, which allows access to a grassy track, which runs under overgrown hawthorns along the top of the field below. After a few pleasant minutes you will reach the boundary of Castle Wood, and the walk changes character. Enter the wood and continue along its northern boundary on an obvious, but overgrown, path. *Buried in the woods you will pass a derelict dwelling, which sports some interesting inscribed brickwork and – unless it falls before you arrive – one last oak window frame hanging tenuously from an upstairs window.* A little way after the ruin the wood broadens out and the path, still running along the inside of the forest boundary, turns left steeply uphill. Walk up the hill. *This is no real hardship as the mixed deciduous woods are lovely, and at the right time of year the ground is covered in bluebells.* As you reach the crest of the hill, the woods thin out into bracken and a gate leads you onto more grazing land.

3 Cross three fields, sticking to the top boundary of the first, and then trending slightly downwards across the next two. As you cross the first stile of this section you approach the highest point of the walk, just 30 metres from the summit of Castle Hill, which lies a quarter of a mile away but is not accessible. *The hills of northern Radnorshire can be studied to their best effect from this point. Although they do not share the drama of the wild lands to the west of Rhayader, Camlo Hill, which has been keeping you company on the right for some time now, and Moel Hywel, which has just come into view, do have their own modest virtues. Camlo is the more substantial of the two, protectively shielding Abbeycwmhir behind a lengthy sweep of green curtain. Moel Hywel is a different creature – of the same height, but more compact and conse-*

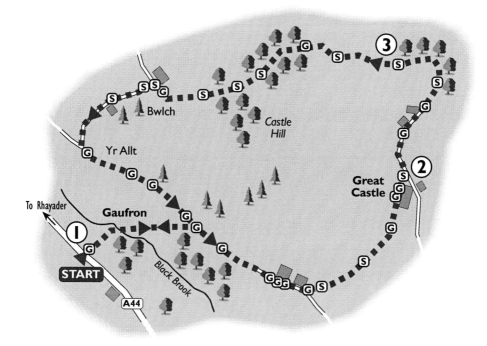

quently with more potential to impress. It has however had most of its wildness removed by modern agriculture, except for a small patch of rough ground hiding in its southern cwm, which is well observed from our present viewpoint. Across the dramatic edges of the Wye Valley, the wind turbines of Bryn Titli have come into view, and behind them you can make out some of the new industrial monsters on Cefn Croes. Quickly, however, they disappear from view, and you enter the next woodland stretch of the walk, Berthabley Wood. A gate allows you to enter the wood, and after a short stretch of woodland path, a stile allows you to exit. You are, however, only in the open field for a very brief stretch until the path, trending very gently downhill, *takes you into Bwlch Wood, which is different in character to the other woods on the walk because the boundaries have been left open and the space underneath the trees is grazed and open.* Enter the wood

next to a broken down stile, and take the downhill path towards the bottom corner of the wood. From this point you can see back across the valley to Gaufron. Keep right, and follow a track next to a field boundary down to the farm of Upper Bwlch, which can be seen nestling below. Passing the farm, turn left over a stile next to some fuel tanks. Go through a small field and enter the last piece of woodland on the walk – this time a block of coniferous forest plantation. Go straight through the conifers on a waymarked track, but instead of exiting through the gate at the bottom, climb up the forest boundary a short way to exit over a stile into the field above. Contour around the field, through some fir trees, to come down onto a track. Turn left, past a quarry, and go through the left hand of the two gates ahead. A short stroll along a grassy track will complete the circuit of Castle Hill, and a right turn will take you back to your car.

5

MAEN SERTH & THE WYE VALLEY (NORTH)

DESCRIPTION A relatively gentle hill walk along clearly marked tracks which returns along a minor road. The full circuit is around nine and a half miles, for which five hours should be allowed. The shorter route is six and a half miles, for which three hours should be ample.

START Rhayader Town Centre. Parking outside of Rhayader can reduce the distance.

1 Leave Rhayader along the B4518, and head up the mountain road towards Aberystwyth. At just over half a mile a road up the mountain road, take the right turn, signposted to Nannerth and proceed gently uphill for less than quarter of a mile. Go through a gate on the left, which marks the beginning of a track across the gorse patched open hillside. In places a choice of routes is offered, but if you wish to keep to the right of way, take the right hand fork every time. This track is a byway open to all traffic, and is sometimes used by off road bikers and 4x4 drivers. Its surface bears the scars of this activity, but is nonetheless easy to follow as it takes a leisurely line up the broad ridge ahead. It initially bears to the right, avoiding a minor elevation on the ridge and following field boundaries which overlook the valley of the Wye. The fields soon give way to a conifer plantation, before the track meanders back to the ridge to make a more resolute assault on the main peak of Esgair Dderw.

2 Follow the track up to Esgair Dderw, making a brief detour, along which others have clearly passed before you, *to admire the standing stone of Maen Serth. This is one of the more impressive and intriguing standing stones of the Elenydd. It is probably of Bronze Age origin, although a cross was cut into one of its faces in the thirteenth century, supposedly to commemorate the murder of the Welsh Prince Einion Clud by the Marcher Lord Roger Mortimer. Alas, the cross is no longer easy to discern amongst the lichens of the weathered stone.* From Maen Serth, return along the obvious trail to the main track and descend to the bwlch immediately to the west. Cross this and head along the track, ignoring a left fork. At the toe of the next hill it is possible to escape to the right, along a bridleway, down into the Wye Valley. Those with limited time or energy will wish to make this initially steep descent which contours around the top of field boundaries to descend steeply again through the farm of Cwmcoch. On hitting the metalled road turn right and follow tarmac along the serene Wye Valley, until it gently climbs back around the foot of the hill you have just climbed and allows obvious access back to Cwmdeuddwr and Rhayader.

3 Those with more time and energy, and who relish open moorland walking, can now abandon the track and climb the other side of the bwlch. The going under foot is easier than a study of the map might suggest, and the scenic rewards are well worth striving for. Keeping the crags above Fergwm to the right wander along the lip of the valley. *The views grow ever more dramatic as progress is made. Across the Wye valley the rocky bulk of Gamallt thrusts upwards with a drama which belies its relatively modest height.* Try to ignore the intrusive turbines on Bryn Titli and descend northwards into the bwlch of Nant y Sarn.

4 As you descend begin to bear left. This will make the inevitable climb out of the other side less of a burden. *You will see the ruins of Lluest Penrhiw across the bwlch to the north.* Climb up to these, pass them, and then turn right at the obvious track.

Lluest-pen-rhiw

Nannerthffrwdd

Cerrig Gwalch

③

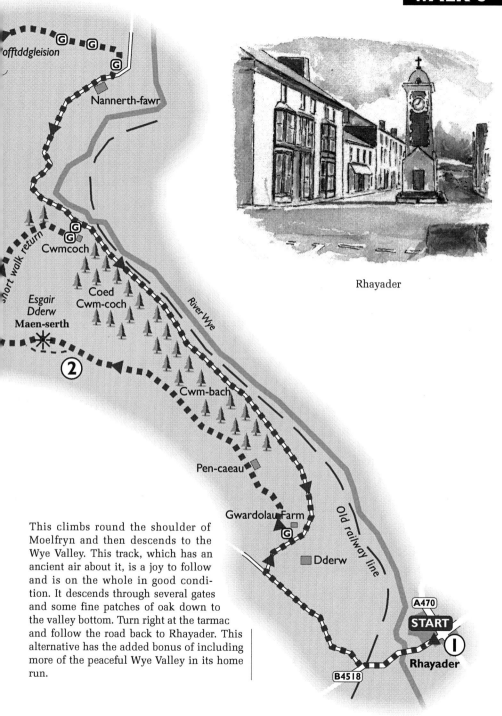

Rhayader

offtddgleision

Nannerth-fawr

short walk return

Cwmcoch

Esgair
Dderw
Maen-serth

Coed
Cwm-coch

River Wye

②

Cwm-bach

Pen-caeau

Gwardolau Farm

Dderw

Old railway line

This climbs round the shoulder of Moelfryn and then descends to the Wye Valley. This track, which has an ancient air about it, is a joy to follow and is on the whole in good condition. It descends through several gates and some fine patches of oak down to the valley bottom. Turn right at the tarmac and follow the road back to Rhayader. This alternative has the added bonus of including more of the peaceful Wye Valley in its home run.

A470

START

Rhayader

B4518

7

A SHORT ROUND FROM LLANWRTHWL

DESCRIPTION A delightful lowland walk, largely through woodland, but with a section of moorland, and a return along a very minor road.
START Llanwrthwl Village. Park outside the church.
DIRECTIONS From Rhayader take the A470 south. Llanwrthwl is signposted on the right after about three miles. Drive into the village, where the church is easily found.

1 From Llanwrthwl head off along the unclassified road next to the church, which heads south along the Wye Valley. It is signposted to Hodrid, and also marked as part of the Wye Valley Walk. Within half a mile you will see a signpost on the right to Craig Llyn, behind which is a sign indicating the route of a public footpath. Follow this, and go through a gate into a field. Head for an obvious gap in a dry stone wall ahead, which will take you across another field and through a gate into woodland. *The woods are a delight to be in. Mossy boulders are scattered around the floor, with bluebells and foxgloves nestling between them (at the right time of year), while overhead a canopy of mature oak, beech, ash and other deciduous trees encloses a most atmospheric scene.* The footpath is just clear enough to follow without too much difficulty, and trends slightly uphill, though never enough to require much exertion. Just when you think you might be getting lost, a wooden post confirms the way, and shortly afterwards you will arrive at a boundary. Climb a stile into some more woodland, this time coniferous forestry. A narrow, overgrown but easily passable path snakes its way through the trees, which are fairly young and not unpleasant. Half-way through this stretch you will cross a rough forest track, on the other side of which you will have to walk left for a few yards to find the continuation of the footpath. Carry on until you reach a stile, which brings you out behind a wonderful Radnorshire barn, with classic slit-like windows, at Cryn Fryn. Go to the right of the farm buildings and locate a gate in the right hand corner of the enclosure. Pass through and follow the grassy, and sometimes muddy, track beyond. The surrounding fields are quite wooded, and the track has an air of redundancy about it. It is nevertheless easy to follow – just keep the fenceline to your left. Before long you will arrive at a footbridge, which will take you across the stream – Nant Cymrun – to a stile. Climb the stile to come out on a track. Don't stay on the track very long, but look for a stile on the right hand side near the stream, cross it and continue upstream through yet more woodland – this time for the most part boggy, with willow and sallow amongst the trees. Crossing a final stile will change the scene, and begin the second half of the walk.

2 You will emerge onto open moorland in the large Cwm cradled behind the Cwmdeuddwr Hills. Immediately opposite is the flank of Y Gamriw, its stepped crest tumbling down into the Wye Valley in uneven leaps and bounds. *Above you is the lip of the vast emptiness of Abergwesyn Common, which merges into the flanks of Drum Ddu, with a series of incised, hanging valleys breaking the contours.* Cross the moorland by following the footpath more or less along the fence line (a slight bank with sheep tracks along it makes for easier going than the reedy land directly next to the fence). This will quickly and easily lead you to a rough track, on which you turn right to reach a metalled road. Turn right here and follow the road, which is very quiet indeed, all the way back to Llanwrthwl.

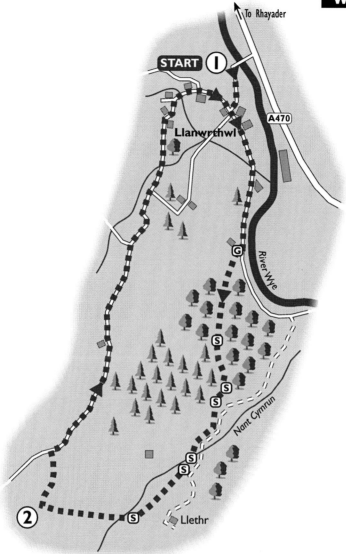

To Rhayader

START ①

A470

Llanwrthwl

River Wye

G

S

S

S

Nant Cymrun

S
S

② S Llethr

About the author, Martin Wright

Martin has lived and worked in Mid Wales for the last twenty years. Originally from Northamptonshire, he fell in love with the Mid Wales hills as a teenager. He studied history at the University of Wales, Lampeter, and has since worked in the field of adult education. He has strong feelings about the Welsh landscape, and has written this book in the hope that it will encourage others to explore and cherish it.

ABBEY-CWM-HIR & CAMLO HILL

DESCRIPTION A circular route centred on the village of Abbey-cwm-hir. The hills around this intriguing place are largely forested, and the walk follows forest paths and tracks for most of its length. There is, however, far more variation than one might expect from a largely coniferous ramble. The high point of the walk is Camlo Hill, which offers a fine withdrawn vantage point from which to view the Elenydd.

START The centre of Abbey-cwm-hir. There is limited parking in the village, but space can usually be found outside the church. Abbey-cwm-hir is well worth a visit in itself, being home to the ruins of a Cistercian Abbey and the burial place of Llywelyn, the last ruler of an independent Wales who was slain in 1282.

DIRECTIONS From the Centre of Rhayader, take the A44 towards Crossgates. Before you leave the town, the road to Abbey-cwm-hir is signposted on the left. The village is about six miles from Rhayader.

I Find the path heading south – through a gate on the opposite side of the road to, and just uphill from, the church. Once through the gate, head around the right hand side of the farm buildings in front of you, and over a stile into the field behind. An indistinct path leads down to the bottom of the field, through a gate and over a bridge. It then climbs briskly up the other side of the valley towards a forest plantation. Climb up towards a stile at the forest boundary, and cross it to enter the forest. The uphill path through the trees is at first obvious, but within a few minutes it breaks out into an extensive section of cleared forest. This is confusing at first, as the path seems to have been obliterated by the felling work. All is however not as bad as it first seems, as following your instincts diagonally will quickly put you back on a more certain track, the path becoming clearer and heading upwards across the hillside through alternate patches of trees and clear-fell. After about a third of a mile you will encounter a potentially confusing set of junctions. To stay on track turn sharp left (uphill) at the first opportunity. This path will quickly deposit you on a broader modern forest track. Turn right, and then take the first (almost immediate) right turn down a more ancient and attractive grass track. This winds gently into a little valley, where before long it emerges onto another bulldozed modern track. If you've negotiated the maze of paths and tracks successfully there will be a small pond hidden behind the scrubby trees immediately in front of you. The way forward is marked by a wooden post, a few yards to the right of the pond (from your direction of arrival). The path goes directly uphill behind the post. It is fairly overgrown and rough under foot, and at times progress is made easier by skipping right into the more mature plantation that grows beside it. Just as the going gets a little too irritating to be truly enjoyable, another wooden post confirms the way, and the path breaks out onto another firm forest track. Cross this, and continue for a short distance along the grass track opposite until you reach the forest boundary. This is the key to the next part of the walk.

2 To the right, a well defined track leads along the forest boundary. Follow this, sticking to the boundary rather than the official bridleway, and make the ascent of Camlo hill. As Camlo summit is won, a 360-degree view opens up. From the top of Camlo Hill continue along the forest boundary, keeping left at the first junction and glancing over your shoulder from time to time at Camlo's handsomely ragged flank. In a short while, at a slightly boggy point on the track, an opportunity is given to turn right and rejoin the official bridleway. Take this, and continue to follow the bridleway downhill until it reaches the road at a gate. Turn left here, and walk along the unclassified road for a short distance until the road turns sharply left. At this point a gate on the right hand side (the right hand of two gates) allows access into the field beyond. There is no signpost, but a bridleway crosses the field. This is indistinct at first, but soon becomes obvious enough as it follows a gentle spur down into the valley bottom. To the right is a secluded fragment

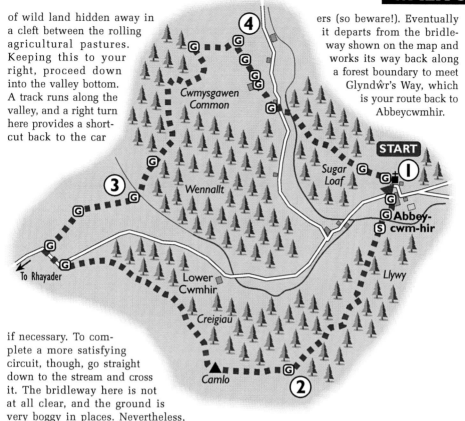

of wild land hidden away in a cleft between the rolling agricultural pastures. Keeping this to your right, proceed down into the valley bottom. A track runs along the valley, and a right turn here provides a short-cut back to the car

ers (so beware!). Eventually it departs from the bridle-way shown on the map and works its way back along a forest boundary to meet Glyndŵr's Way, which is your route back to Abbeycwmhir.

if necessary. To complete a more satisfying circuit, though, go straight down to the stream and cross it. The bridleway here is not at all clear, and the ground is very boggy in places. Nevertheless, a dry foot traverse of the valley bottom is possible, and the way out becomes apparent by heading along the forest boundary towards a corner. A gate allows escape from the boggy ground and provides access to the forest beyond.

3 Once through the gate, you will join another forest track that leads up a valley towards Cwmysgawen Common. Continue up the valley onto the common, now all forestry land. On the top, route finding can become a little confusing. Felling has obliterated the obvious bridleway, so it makes more sense to continue along the forest track, ignoring all left turns until a narrow path, which is marked by a wooden post, appears on the left. Follow this path downhill, gently at first and then more steeply. The track becomes ever more definite, and in places shows sign of use by off-road bik-

4 Glyndŵr's Way is well signposted, and shouldn't present any route finding problems. Turn out right onto the track, passing through a gate, and follow it through some fields. At the end of the third field you will cross a little bridge. Turn right immediately after this, through a gate, and follow the way-marks up the field ahead and down past the farm of Cwmysgawen. Take a right hand gate out of the yard of Cwmysgawen, and follow the path through a field and out to the road, by some decrepit looking sheds. Glyndŵr's Way continues over the road, more or less opposite, in the form, initially at any rate, of a sunken and clearly ancient track. Follow this down into a dip, across a stream and then up over the bwlch that separates the hills cradling Abbeycwmhir. You will come out behind the church in the centre of the village.

GARREG LWYD, BRYN TITLI WINDFARM & THE WYE VALLEY

DESCRIPTION A hill climb, with a flat and leisurely return along the Wye Valley. The objective of the walk is a thought provoking visit to the turbines at Bryn Titli. The total distance is just over seven and a half miles, for which four hours should be allowed.

START Pont Marteg Car Park

DIRECTIONS From Rhayader take the A470 north towards Llangurig. Pont Marteg car park is just off the first right hand turn (signposted to Gilfach Nature Reserve), just under three miles out of Rhayader.

Turn out of the car park away from the main road and towards the visitor centre of Gilfach Nature Reserve. Follow the road around something of a mountain spur on the left, and pass the entrance to Gilfach on the right. Do not go down to Gilfach but continue for another quarter of a mile until a track leads off sharply on the left. Leave the road and follow the track uphill until it forks, then take the left fork through two gates. This is marked as a public footpath on the maps, although on the ground it is a hard based landrover track, which leads to the house of Blaen Riad. At the house, follow the hairpin upwards through two gates, and continue steeply to join another track which comes from the right. As the route circumnavigates the peak of Yr Wylorn, over 100 metres above, it reveals dramatic views of the rugged interior of Cwm Marcheini Fawr. Eventually you will arrive at a gate, which gives access to the plateau above. The track makes its way through a number of gates across intensively grazed fields, avoiding an elevation to the left. After crossing a bwlch it skirts around the summit of Garreg Lwyd, which makes its presence felt on the left as a swell of wilder looking moor above the 'improved' fields.

2 *The view from the top of Garreg Lwyd is both beautiful and shocking. The Radnor Forest and the Black Mountains give substance to the south easterly vista, and your eye will pick out the peaks of the Brecon Beacons, sticking up like teeth from behind the Elenydd, as it works its way eastwards eventually to Pumlumon. To the north however are the 22 wind turbines that cover the plateau of Bryn Titli. Not too far behind them are another fifty or so at Carno, and, to the east, over a hundred at Llandinam. 39 even larger turbines have recently been added to the northern Elenydd at Cefn Croes, to the north west of you, and there are plans in the pipeline for hundreds more across the Cambrian Mountains. If such plans materialise, the Elan Valley will be a haven of peace within a largely industrialised landscape!* With this provocative thought in mind, continue along the path, pass through a gate and head over to the nearest turbine. Turn left along the access track and follow the hard surfaced bridleway through more gates down to the main road in the valley below.

3 Pass by an unwelcoming NO PARKING sign, which seems to have been put up to deter access to the windfarm, and turn left at the main road. Cross the road and almost immediately turn right down a minor road (signposted Dernol), which heads down towards the River Wye. Cross the Wye and then take a sharp left turn, followed swiftly by another left turn. The road then runs alongside the Wye, keeping close company with the river for just over two miles of delightful and easy walking. After a while the surroundings become wooded and the road begins to rise away from the river. At its highest point a signposted footpath breaks off on the left through woodland. Follow this, through several gates, down to a delightfully situated footbridge across the Wye. A traverse of the bridge, followed quickly by the main road, will see you back at your car.

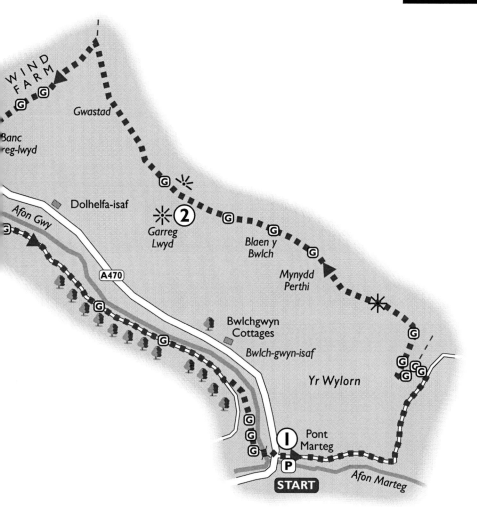

WIND FARM

Ⓖ Ⓖ

Banc
reg-lwyd

Gwastad

Afon Gwy

Ⓖ

Dolhelfa-isaf

Ⓖ ☀

☀ ②
Garreg
Lwyd

Ⓖ

A470

Blaen y
Bwlch

Ⓖ

Ⓖ

Mynydd
Perthi

✳

Ⓖ

Bwlchgwyn
Cottages

Ⓖ

Ⓖ

Bwlch-gwyn-isaf

Yr Wylorn

ⒼⒼ Ⓖ
ⒼⒼ

Ⓖ

Ⓖ
Ⓖ
Ⓖ

ⓘ
Pont
Marteg

Ⓟ

START

Afon Marteg

CRUGYN CI

DESCRIPTION A very varied walk indeed. The route follows tarmac, woodland paths and mountain trails, as well as traversing open moor. Six miles in all, the route will take around three hours.

START Roadside parking space at 952688 on the mountain road from Rhayader to Aberystwyth.

I Walk up-valley from the car, gradually rising above Gwyn Llyn which lies in the basin below. Take the first left turn, and follow the public right of way past the rather forbidding PRIVATE sign down through the woods. Cross Nant Gwyn Llyn, and continue to Treheslog Farm, as on **Walk 2**. Instead of turning back towards Rhayader immediately after the farm, however, continue along the footpath. At first the route is not at all obvious. Be sure to fully cross the farmyard and follow the fence line which heads up the mountain. From the farmyard it is hidden behind a hedge, but once found the path is good and clearly marked. Continue along the path, passing the ruins of an old barn, until it comes to an obvious junction.

2 The downhill route is barred by a permanently closed gate and looks rather overgrown in the summer, but we are concerned with the uphill route. This doubles back fairly obviously and climbs the hills alongside a patch of sessile oak. As it climbs the route changes character. The oak gives way to rocky hillside, and as the path winds upwards, a fine view into the Wye Valley begins to open out. The steep climb is not as painful as it at first threatens, and before long it levels out onto the plateau. Follow it, as it contours around the flow of the land and arrives at the lonely ruin of Pant y Llyn, with its forlorn stand of trees. From Pant y Llyn, strike off in a westerly direction across the open moor. After not much more than a quarter of a mile you will hit an obvious track. From here the outcroppy hump of Crugyn Ci is the most obvious feature of the plateau,

and it is simply a matter of choice as to when you wish to leave the track and make your way up to it. *Crugyn Ci is an excellent place to rest and take lunch. Shelter is easy enough to find, if needed, and the view takes in most of the Elenydd plateau. Pumlumon forms the northern horizon, while the Cwmdeuddwr Hills unfold to the south. All is space and peace.*

3 Once you've had enough of Crugyn Ci (for now) descend back to the main track, turn right and follow it briefly until a narrow but obvious footpath strikes off to the left and cuts across the head of Cwm Blyn-bren. (If you start losing height significantly, you've gone too far). After half a mile this joins a bridleway which has climbed out of the valley below. Follow the bridleway for over half a mile across the moorland until it descends into Cwm-nant. This section is potentially complicated as there is in fact a maze of paths on the moor. The thing to remember is to keep bearing left. For the most part the path is surprisingly firm, rocky even, underfoot, although the odd quagmire will require evasive action. Finally the route bears to the left of a rocky knoll and begins to descend in earnest. Head down into Cwm Nant until there is an obvious left turn which cuts back across the infant valley, crossing the stream to briefly climb out of the other side. Take this, but instead of being drawn back up onto the moor by the adjoining paths take the sharp right turn which heads directly downhill. Follow the path through a gate into the forest plantation which lies ahead. Continue steeply downhill through the dense trees, until you reach a gate at the bottom.

4 From here the most attractive looking route on the map is the footpath which runs north through the woods beneath

Crugyn Ci
533m

③

Bwlch Croesnewydd

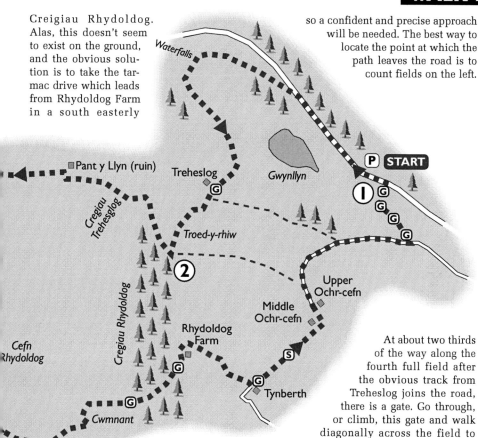

Creigiau Rhydoldog. Alas, this doesn't seem to exist on the ground, and the obvious solution is to take the tarmac drive which leads from Rhydoldog Farm in a south easterly

so a confident and precise approach will be needed. The best way to locate the point at which the path leaves the road is to count fields on the left.

direction back to the end of the public road. Once on the road, turn left and go through the gate to follow a lane uphill between the fields. This is a road used as a public path, although I doubt it could be traversed even by the most intrepid of off-road drivers! It is therefore perfect for the pedestrian. Follow this until it passes through a most attractive set of former farm buildings at Uper Ochr Cefn and bears left to reach tarmac again. Follow the pleasant lane after the buildings as it works its way around the hillside and begins to double back towards Rhayader along a forest boundary. Your car will now be directly across the valley. In order to reach it you will need to traverse the shallow valley on public footpaths. These are not signposted

At about two thirds of the way along the fourth full field after the obvious track from Treheslog joins the road, there is a gate. Go through, or climb, this gate and walk diagonally across the field to its corner. Go through another gate and follow the field boundary on the right until you can get to the stream. Crossing the stream will provide some sport to end the day, before you follow another field boundary on the right up to a gate, on the other side of which you will find your car.

Pant y Llyn

15

CWM ELAN MINE & MOELFRYN

DESCRIPTION An initially easy walk along the side of Garreg Ddu Reservoir which gains interest as it climbs up to the ruins of Cwm Elan Mine and then onto the open tops above. The distance is four and a half miles, for which two and a half hours should be enough..

START Car park below Pen y Garreg Dam. There is adequate parking around Pen y Garreg Dam. Either park at the main Dam car park (915673) or at the marked parking places on the roadside (915672).

I If you have parked at the dam you will need to follow the road right out of the car park for a short distance. From the roadside parking lots you will simply need to cross the road. Either way, pass through the gate on the hairpin corner. Follow the track below a forestry plantation and above the upper reaches of Garreg Ddu Reservoir. After less than a mile the track will bring you to the farm buildings of Tynllidiart. Pass around the back of the house on a clearly marked path and proceed across the reedy fields. The path becomes slightly less distinct, although remains easy enough to follow. Continue into a patch of deciduous woodland and descend close to the edge of the reservoir. After a short distance the path bears to the right to allow for the entry of Nant Methan into the reservoir.

2 As the path begins to climb away from the water's edge, and just before it leaves the woods, there is an obvious track on the right. Follow this along the bottom of the woodland up into Cwm Methan. As the track leaves the woods, the ruins of Cwm Elan Mine come into view. *The site is worthy of careful exploration and consists of wheel-pits, platforms, shafts, a buddle, a smithy and the mine offices. The mine was worked from the 1790s to the 1870s, although most of the remains date from the last few years of its working life. The incongruous red brick building next to the mine offices is in fact a dwelling built by Birmingham Corporation to house estate workers in the 1890s.* After the mine, the track peters out into a path, which climbs up the right hand side of the valley. Keep climbing until the gradient eases. The sheds of Cae Bleanmethan come into view on the left, and the path eventually breaks out onto the shoulder of Moelfryn, where it becomes a little more definite in form before it joins another track. Turn right here and follow the track across the top of Moelfryn. In order to stand on the summit proper a very brief diversion to the right is necessary, *but whichever route is taken the views north over the upper Elan Valley and across to Pumlumon are impressive.*

3 Once Moelfryn is traversed, the track begins to drop down the broad ridge until it reaches the corner of a forestry plantation. A direct descent down the forest boundary is possible but not recommended, as it is very steep and numerous protruding tree roots invite a head over heel tumble towards disaster. For a safer way down follow the track along the forest boundary until it splits, with one branch disappearing into the forest and the other heading back uphill around the head of the valley below. Ignore both, and strike off in a southerly direction across the hillside. As the ground begins to steepen you should pick up a path, which heads back down in broad zigzags to Tynllidiart. Follow this, turning left at the house to amble back along the track to your car.

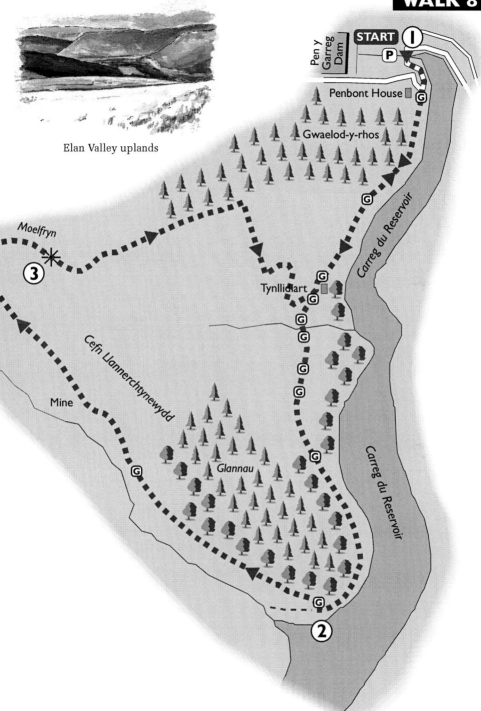

Elan Valley uplands

CABAN COCH RESERVOIR

DESCRIPTION A mostly straightforward walk around one of the Elan reservoirs. The way out is along paths and involves some hill climbing, and the way back is a gentle amble along tarmac. A walk of seven miles, for which three and a half hours should be allowed.

START Elan Valley Visitor Centre

DIRECTIONS Take the B4518 out of Rhayader, towards Elan Village. The Elan Valley Visitor Centre is clearly signposted.

1 *The Elan Valley Visitor Centre, where there are adequate car parking facilities, boasts a range of attractions, including exhibitions about the valley and its water catchment scheme, a tea and gift shop and an impressive location beneath Caban Coch Dam.* Having enjoyed all of these (or perhaps saving the tea room for the way back), leave the visitor centre and turn immediately right across a narrow bridge which crosses the Elan. Immediately over the bridge take the right hand track, which soon forks left and climbs to the top of Caban Coch Dam. *This, the first in a chain of dams up the Elan, is as good a point as any to ponder the engineering achievement of the dam builders. It took thirteen years to complete the ambitious scheme, and over 50,000 workers went through the Corporation's books during that time. Over 106 million gallons of water now flow daily by gravity along 73 miles of pipe to Birmingham.*

2 From the dam turn your back on the valley beneath you and follow the obvious path along the side of the reservoir. *It is soon difficult to believe that the so often bustling Visitor Centre is just minutes around the corner.* The path contours above the water's edge, where it is initially hemmed in under the steep crags of Craig Cnwch, but the hillside above soon becomes gentler and oak covered. After just under two thirds of a mile the path contours away from the reservoir to

climb the side of the valley of Nant-y-Gro. Follow it along the boundary of a forest plantation which runs obliquely up the hillside. The worst of the climb is over by the time the path breaks away from the forest boundary to make a direct assault on the less steep land above, and another few minutes will bring you to the ruins of Ty'n y Pant.

3 From Ty'n y Pant an obvious track leads southwards out of the hollow which gave the house its Welsh name. Follow this track, crossing two easily traversable fords, as it contours back to the Forest boundary. Initially climbing around the broad spur which sprawls north from Gro Hill, you soon begin to descend, along the forest edge for most of the way. Head down through several gates, until you join an even more definite track near the banks of Dolymynach Reservoir. Bear to the left and follow the track until it turns to tarmac at the farm of Llanerch Cawr. Pass the farm, and turn right at the first opportunity over a small road bridge, to cross the Afon Claerwen.

4 Head up to the tarmac above and turn right. Get off the tarmac at the first opportunity by taking a path on your left, which leads up through a gate into some forestry. Proceed on a clear track through the forest for almost two miles, going straight across the first junction. After almost two miles you will reach an obvious crossroads, next to a stream. Turn right here and head downhill to come out at the road. Cross the reservoir on an attractive viaduct near the chapel (which was built by Birmingham Corporation to replace the one they flooded), and turn right. You can avoid walking on tarmac and dodging traffic by passing through a gate on your right as you leave the viaduct. This gives you access to the Elan Valley Way, which runs along the

Craig-y-Mynach

Dolymyna Reser

Llannerch Fawr

bed of the railway that was constructed to aid the building of the dams and will take you back to the Visitor Centre.

START ① P

Elan Valley Visitor Centre

Dam

Coed y Foel

④

Coed Aberelen

Caban-coch Reservoir

Ty'n y Pant

②

Graig Fawr

Coed Lan-fraith

Dam

③

GARREG DDU RESERVOIR

DESCRIPTION A straightforward and largely flat walk around one of the Elan reservoirs. On the way out the route follows tracks and footpaths, and on the way back it follows a tarmac road. A gentle walk of just under six miles, which can be completed in two and a half hours.
START Car park below Pen y Garreg Dam.
DIRECTIONS From Rhayader take the B4518 to Elan Village. Pass the Visitor Centre and follow the road around the reservoir system. The car park is at the top of the second reservoir. There is adequate parking around Pen y Garreg Dam. Either park at the main Dam car park (915673) or at the marked parking places on the roadside (915672). If you have parked at the dam you will need to follow the road right out of the car park for a short distance.

I From the roadside parking lots you will simply need to cross the road and pass through the gate on the hairpin corner opposite. Follow the track below the forestry plantation and above the upper reaches of Garreg Ddu Reservoir. After less than a mile the track will bring you to the farm buildings of Tynllidiart. Pass around the back of the

house on a clearly marked path and proceed across the reedy fields. The path becomes slightly less distinct, although remaining easy enough to follow. Continue along it as it enters a patch of deciduous woodland and descends very close to the edge of the reservoir. After a short distance the path bears to the right to allow for the entry of Nant Methan, and its containing valley, into the reservoir.

2 Nant Methan homes the abandoned buildings and workings of the Elan mine, which is visited on **Walk 8**. Once the Methan is traversed the path migrates again to the shore of the reservoir. Continue through mixed deciduous woods until it strikes a hardcore track. Enjoy the easy going as the track circumnavigates the southern arm of Garreg Ddu. As it doubles back towards Garreg Ddu Dam the woodland changes from broadleaves to conifers, then to a patch of rather ugly clearfell. Once you are alongside the clearfell, the dam is only a matter of minutes ahead.

3 Cross the dam and turn left. You can avoid the tarmac and passing traffic by taking the Elan Valley Way, which runs between the road and the reservoir. After about two and a half miles of easy walking you will reach your car.

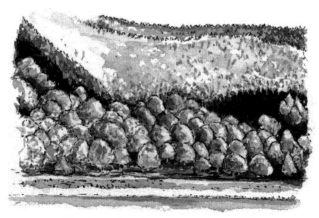

Mixed woodlands seen across Carreg Ddu

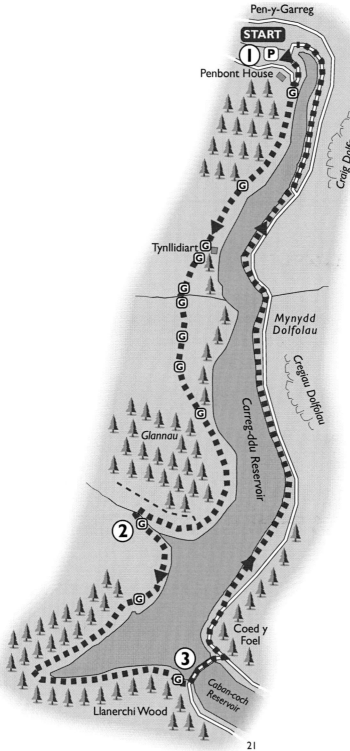

Pen-y-Garreg

START

I   P

Penbont House

G

G

Craig Dolfaenog

Tynllidiart

G
G

G
G

Mynydd
Dolfolau

G

Cregiau Dolfolau

G

G

Glannau

Carreg-ddu Reservoir

2   G

G

Coed y
Foel

3

G

Caban-coch
Reservoir

Llanerchi Wood

WALK 11

PEN Y GARREG RESERVOIR, CRUGYN CI & THE ROMAN CAMP

DESCRIPTION A walk of varying character. The first section is a flat wander on a well maintained path along the side of Pen y Garreg Reservoir, and the second section involves traversing open moorland on bridleways which are easy to follow. A walk of just under seven and a half miles, which can be completed in three and a half hours.

START Car park at Craig Goch Dam

DIRECTIONS From Rhayader take the B4518 to Elan Village. Drive up the Elan reservoir system. The car park is at the top of the third reservoir.

1 From the Gothic dam at Craig Goch, take the obvious path south above the banks of Pen y Garreg Reservoir, *which follows the bed of an old tramway built to aid the construction of the dam. It is now a popular tourist route equipped with picnic tables and waymarks.* Continue south below the wonderful oak woodland, with the water of the reservoir on the right until you arrive at Pen y Garreg Dam. *This stretch of walking does not have the feel of lonely remoteness that some of the other routes boast, and on fine summer weekends you will most likely be greeting a constant stream of people.* Nevertheless it will provide half an hour of thoroughly enjoyable brisk walking.

2 At the dam continue along the track, through woodland, remembering to look down over your right shoulder at the impressive engineering feat behind you. The track soon becomes metalled, and then offers the opportunity to double back up the hillside along a small plantation boundary. Take this,

and continue to Pen y Garreg Farm. Shortly after the farm a bridleway strikes off to the right, tackling the hill slope in a more direct manner. Take the right turn and after a couple of enclosed fields the terrain opens out into grassland. Follow the track as it obliquely climbs the hillside above Cwm Blymbren, and stay left at the obvious branch. Further climbing will bring you up onto the plateau, where it is worth making a detour from the path to tarry on the outcrop of Crugyn Ci.

3 Rejoin the bridleway and continue as it gradually descends towards the mountain road which runs out of Rhayader and crosses the hills to Cwmystwyth. Turn left at the road, walk along it for about a third of a mile and then take a bridleway which heads back across the moorland on the left. Climbing up onto the flanks of Esgair Perfedd the track goes through the site of a Roman marching camp. Alas, there is little to be seen from ground level today and the camp is best appreciated from the air.

4 The track continues, straightforward to follow, across Esgair Perfedd until it descends to Craig Goch Dam and reunites you with your car.

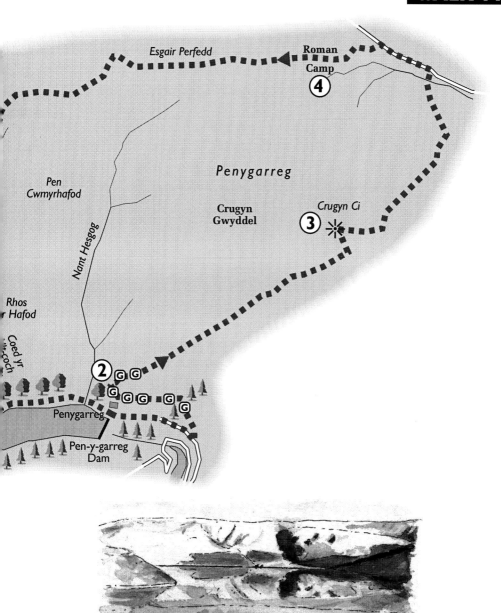

Esgair Perfedd

Roman Camp
④

Penygarreg

Pen Cwmyrhafod

Crugyn Gwyddel

Crugyn Ci
③ ☀

Nant Hesgog

Rhos r Hafod

Coed yr -coch

②ⓖⓖ
ⓖⓖⓖ ⓖ ⓖ

Penygarreg

Pen-y-garreg Dam

Craig Goch Reservoir

AROUND NANT MADOG

DESCRIPTION A 5½ mile hill walk through beautiful terrain with some fairly steep sections, but also plenty of gentle rambling. The first section passes through farmland on footpaths, and the second explores the open country above.

START

Elan Valley Visitor Centre.

DIRECTIONS

Take the B4518 out of Rhayader, towards Elan Village. The Elan Valley Visitor Centre is clearly signposted.

1 From the Visitor Centre head back up to the Rhayader road. On the right you will find a gate, which allows you onto a cycle track, thus allowing you to avoid walking on the road. Follow the cycle track, passing by houses and an impressive chapel, until you arrive at a sewage works on your right. Leave the track here, cross the road and pass through the gate of Llanfadog-uchaf Farm. Head towards the house, but take a sharp right turn before you reach the house, and climb over a waymarked stile. Go through the gate directly ahead of you, and head along the upper boundary of a field, *which, if you are walking this in the early summer, will be carpeted in wild flowers.* Continue, across another stile and through another gate until you arrive at Lower Llanfadog Farm. In walking across two fields, you have clearly crossed an old linguistic boundary! Go through the farmyard, and turn right, around the house. *As you pass the farm you will see a fine old chimney standing behind the house – which was presumably once attached to the farm or whatever building previously occupied its place. It is an impressive architectural remnant, and clearly of some antiquity.* Bear right out of the farmyard, and then take a waymarked left turn almost immediately. A good track climbs upwards from here, initially through trees, and then even more directly uphill between field boundaries. Follow this all the way up to a gate that opens out onto a very minor road. Oak woodland entices you across the track, and if you turn left and then take the right hand fork that quickly comes into sight you can walk up into it. The large Private Road sign that is pinned to a tree at the start of the track does not apply to pedestrians, as the route is a public footpath, so ignore it and head heedlessly up through the trees. *The going here is delightful. Nant yr Haidd – a tributary of Nant Madog, which itself runs into the Elan – busily chatters from the wooded dingle to your left while oak trees reach out their branches over your head.* Before long you will climb out of the woods and the open hills above will begin to reveal themselves. Follow the track beneath craggy hillsides all the way to the dwelling of Nant yr Haidd. Pass directly in front of the house and turn immediately to the right alongside a collection of sheds. Above the sheds, the track bears left and goes through a medley of gates until eventually you break out onto open country. *You can now roam at will, and forget all about fences, gates and stiles!*

2 This part of the Elan watershed is exquisitely beautiful. *The scenery is soft, but with a hard edge. The moorland breaks like waves, each with its own craggy crest of outcrop. The land swells around you and falls away below into a gentle half-wooded hollow, which cradles Nant Madog. Underfoot is a springy bilberry bush carpet, and to your left is a majestic, but deteriorating, dry stone wall.* Looking across the wall you can survey the next part of the walk, which negotiates the top of the cwm and heads across to the obvious hump beyond. The best way across is initially to stick to the path you are on as it works away from the wall and fence-line. Its line is quite clear on the ground, discretely scored into the undergrowth by vehicle tracks. After a short distance you will see a concrete marker – *an Elan Estate boundary stone.* Keep heading towards this until you reach a track, which is clear on the ground, turns left and allows you to proceed with ease through the undergrowth, which is now dominated by heather – a *welcome change from the Molinia grass that dominates much of the Elenydd.* Descend slightly into the bwlch, alongside a line of craggy outcrops to your right, and through some boggy ground. An Elan Valley Estate waymark indicates the line of the public footpath that heads back down to Elan Village, and provides a way out of the rather complex network of tracks that serve the head of the bwlch. Go left at the waymark, but leave the path after a short while (at the next waymark) and head across the open moor towards its summit. A short and pleasant climb through the heather and grassland will get you to the 480 metre summit, known as Carreg Bica. *A pile of stones adds definition to the rounded grassy hump, and the views are splendid.*

3 Retrace your steps back to the footpath, turn right and follow it downhill. The path is quite distinct on the ground and occasionally waymarked. Descend until you reach the lower limits of the open country at a gate. Do not go through the gate, but continue along the fenceline, which steepens as the path passes a woodland enclosure and then proceeds in a dog-leg down the last steep sections of hillside. The path eventually brings you to the back

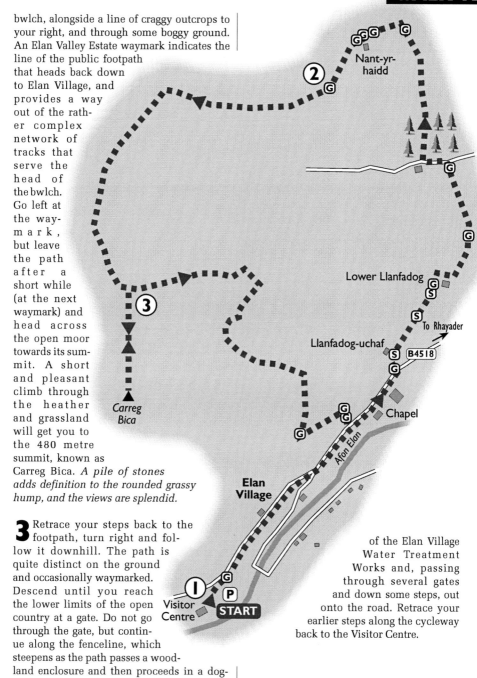

of the Elan Village Water Treatment Works and, passing through several gates and down some steps, out onto the road. Retrace your earlier steps along the cycleway back to the Visitor Centre.

CARN GAFALLT

DESCRIPTION The heathery moorland of Carn Gafallt swells to the south west of Rhayader, and is cut of from the surrounding upland by the River Elan to the north and the Dulas to the south. This walk takes you up over the moor and back along the enchanting Dulas valley. The route is just under 8 miles, allowing for some wandering to the top of Clap Round, and will take up to four hours.

START Llanwrthwl. There is limited car parking space in front of the church.

DIRECTIONS From Rhayader take the A470 south. Llanwrthwl is signposted on the right after about three miles. Drive into the village, where the church will be obvious.

I Leave the village of Llanwrthwl by following the road you arrived on. Shortly after passing the left turn to Penrhos, and the old schoolhouse on the right, a public footpath (signed as part of the Wye Valley Walk) breaks off on the right. Head upwards along its sunken bed, until you reach the farm of Dolgai and the road. Turn left and then immediately right to climb the hill on a well maintained track, which is again signposted as part of the Wye Valley Walk. This zig-zags up the hill and through woodland. *Look out for the artistically abandoned van in the woods*, and continue along the track, through several gates until it passes the farm of Cefn on the left.

2 Not long after Cefn, and after another gate, the track splits. The Wye Valley Walk bears off to the right and quickly begins to descend back into the Valley which gives it its mission. Abandon it, and continue along the left fork. This flanks a gentle hump of plateau on its right hand side and heads off in a south westerly direction across the heathery moorland. Keep going, ignoring another two tracks which join the route from the right. Shortly after the second of them, the bridleway begins to follow the foot of a small slope on the moor. Continue until you see a signpost indicating another route

– this time less distinct – on the left. The left branch of this path provides a route back, but before you do this a wander around on top of Carn Gafallt will prove rewarding.

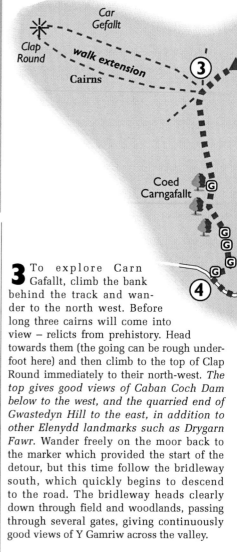

3 To explore Carn Gafallt, climb the bank behind the track and wander to the north west. Before long three cairns will come into view – relics from prehistory. Head towards them (the going can be rough underfoot here) and then climb to the top of Clap Round immediately to their north-west. *The top gives good views of Caban Coch Dam below to the west, and the quarried end of Gwastedyn Hill to the east, in addition to other Elenydd landmarks such as Drygarn Fawr.* Wander freely on the moor back to the marker which provided the start of the detour, but this time follow the bridleway south, which quickly begins to descend to the road. The bridleway heads clearly down through field and woodlands, passing through several gates, giving continuously good views of Y Gamriw across the valley.

4 The bridleway reaches the road at a final wooden gate. Pass through this and turn left. Follow the delightfully quiet back road along the valley of the Dulas all the way back to Llanwrthwl. About three miles of gentle walking will get you back to your car.

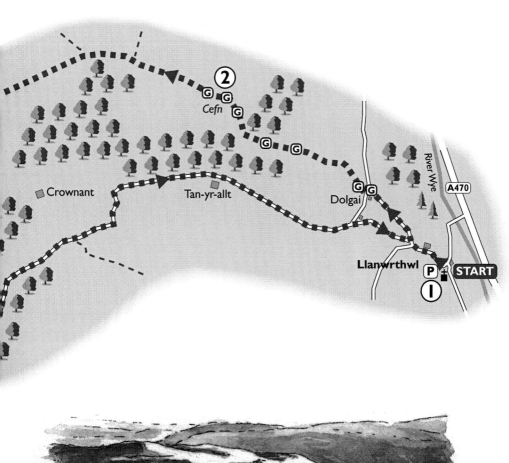

Crownant Tan-yr-allt Cefn Dolgai Llanwrthwl START River Wye A470 (2)

Cairns on Carn gefallt

THE LLANWRTHWL SKYLINE

Y Gamriw & Drum Ddu

DESCRIPTION A fairly challenging hill walk, mostly across open country, which climbs to over 600 metres. Navigation skills are necessary in bad weather or poor visibility. The walk can be split in two, if desired, by using the road from Llanwrthwl as an escape or approach route
START Llanwrthwl Village.
DIRECTIONS Park outside the church. From Rhayader take the A470 south. Llanwrthwl is signposted on the right after about three miles. Drive into the village, where the church is easily found.

I Leave your car outside the church at Llanwrthwl, but carry on walking along the road you have come in on. Take the first left hand turn (signposted to Pen Rhos) and follow the road past a grand red house with an enormous beech tree in the garden. Immediately after the house take a right hand turn along a bridleway to Dol Iago. Follow this track, through several gates, all the way to the farm. At the farm turn left and find a gate behind, which takes you into some forestry. Continue gently uphill until you reach a gate at the top of the forest. Pass through this to access the open hillside. At first the path contours around the hill through bracken and patches of scrub woodland. *The atmosphere is idyllic, you are only just beginning to climb out of the Wye Valley, but the hillside has an aura of wildness blended with softness that is, in my experience, unique to the hills of this region.* After contouring for a short distance, take the first opportunity to strike off right up the steep hillside. A track rises in a dog-leg up the worst of the steepness, and before long you are climbing the trackless, but well defined north ridge of Y Gamriw. The gradient eases, the vegetation thins out and a series of cairns confirms – without any real necessity – that you are on course. Simply follow the ridge all the way to the summit of Y Gamriw.

2 *Once you have enjoyed the top of Y Gamriw, to which (on the right day) there are few comparable pleasures,* carry on directly until you pick up a path that cuts back steeply down the bilberry-clad slope of Rhiw Saeson. This is open country, so you can roam where you please, but the path offers the most sedate way down the slope. Head down into the expansive bwlch beneath you, and across it, crossing a rough track at the halfway point. The whole place has an ancient feel to it. It is littered with cairns and standing stones, and in the hollow below are ancient field systems. *The more recent works of man seem far away. Thankfully, this land is in the hands of the National Trust, held, we are told by a plaque further down the track, in honour of all those who have given their lives for the United Kingdom. That thought adds even more gravity to a place where the weight of the past is, anyway, felt in the air around you.* Climb directly up the slope in front of you, passing a series of cairns. 140 metres of gentle but persistent climbing will get you to the whaleback top of Drum Ddu and its broken-down quartz-speckled monument, *Carn y Geifr – the Cairn of the Goats. The Radnor Forest is clearly visible to the east, and the Cwmdeuddwr Hills to the north and west, but Drum Ddu is also a good vantage point to view the soft, lonely and little known hills of southern Radnorshire – Bruce Chatwin's 'Black Hill' (from a book set in the hill farms of the Welsh Borders, focusing on the relationship between twin brothers who grow up isolated from the course of the twentieth century). Make a mental note to visit them on another day. You will not be disappointed.*

Y Gamriw
604
2
599

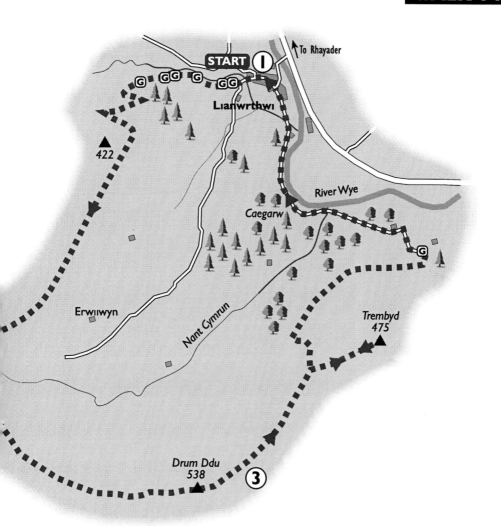

3 Doubtless reluctantly, you will now need to head back to the valley. Continue along the very broad ridge of Drum Ddu until you begin to descend significantly. Bear left here, taking care not to wander off the wrong side of the hill, which is easier than it sounds. You may wish to extend the trip by continuing to the hump of Trembyd, which lies across a shallow bwlch *and gives some good views down the Wye Valley.* Either way, leave the mountain by taking a path

from the bwlch, which snakes down Rhiw Llanwrthwl, until it swings round to the right, above some woodland, to take you all the way to the toe of the hill. As with the lower slopes of Gamriw, the going is delightful through scrub and patches of scattered woodland. Eventually the path, which turns into a bridleway, joins the Wye Valley Walk. Turn left, pass through a gate back onto a metalled road, and follow the road up the Wye Valley back to Llanwrthwl and your car.

WALK 15

BETWEEN CLAERWEN & ELAN

DESCRIPTION An extremely varied and interesting walk, which explores the sides of two very contrasting reservoirs as well as some quintessential pieces of Elenydd plateau and two contrasting valleys. **Avoid misty weather!**
START Claerwen Dam.
DIRECTIONS Head out from Rhayader on the Elan Village road. Pass the village and visitor centre, and continue past the first dam. Turn left at the road bridge by the chapel (signposted to Claerwen), and continue all the way to the Dam, taking a right hand turn (signposted as a dead end) to arrive at the top of the dam.

The huge Dam on the Claerwen is the newest and largest of the region's waterworks. It was opened in 1952 and holds back a reservoir with a capacity almost as great as all the Elan reservoirs put together. Unlike the Elan dams, however, Claerwen is made of concrete, the masonry exterior being a façade. From the top of the dam follow a track that continues up the northern side of the reservoir (ie. not crossing the dam). The Claerwen Reservoir is quite different in atmosphere from its neighbours on the Elan. Even Craig Coch, the most northerly and bleakest of the Elan reservoirs, does not approach the stern countenance of Claerwen. The scale is huge and the surrounding hills have an almost savage aura. The dam is placed right in the heart of some of the wildest country in Mid Wales, and you can feel the remoteness in the air. Even with a strip of tarmac connecting it with the outside world and the gaggle of holidaymakers that find their way to the dam in the summer, the area beyond Claerwen remains lonely territory, far detached from the everyday haunts of mankind. Walk into the apparent wilderness along the side of the reservoir. Go around the first inlet, the valley of the Dyfnant, and continue along to the top of a second. At this point leave the track and head up the valley of Nant y Gadair on a grassy track. Continue to the end of this track and then strike off towards the remains of what appears to be a dwelling and a sheepfold (ignoring the Elan Estate waymark which would send you to the right). Follow the valley immediately beyond the sheepfold, and make your way gradually onto the Elenydd plateau. *With every step the sky seems to expand until you are up on a large shallow bwlch, and all is space.*

2 The aim is to cross the plateau, and join an abandoned watercourse beyond, which will take you onto the next stage of the walk. This appears simple, but the nature of the plateau lends itself to aimless wandering in circles if one doesn't pay sufficient attention to route finding. In misty weather you'd be best advised to take a compass bearing, but in clear weather the best thing to do is to look at the hills opposite and proceed in line with the most obvious nipple-like protuberance on the horizon (which is Crugyn Ci, visited on **Walks 7 & 11**). As you cross the bwlch the land swells to the left into a very low pancake-like bluff. Keep this to your left and begin to head down into the shallow valley opposite. Before descending very far you will arrive at the abandoned watercourse. At first this is only very faintly evident on the ground, but as you contour round to the right its course becomes clearer. Contour all the way around the hillside on the watercourse, which provides a good path in places but is non-existent or boggy in others, until you arrive at the shoulder of Moelfryn. Here you will find a track, along which you turn right and head towards a lonely workstation on the edge of Cae Blaenmethan. Turn left at the sheep station, along a boggy track, and make your way down into the Valley of Nant Methan. The descent requires care in one or two places, particularly in wet weather, so don't get too distracted by the beauty of your surroundings, which become softer as you descend. Pass through a gate, which lies down to the left of a grassy track that is unfortunately blocked by a fence, into the lower reaches of the valley, passing the remains of Cwm Elan Mine (described in **Walk 8**). Keep to the left hand side of the valley, rather than

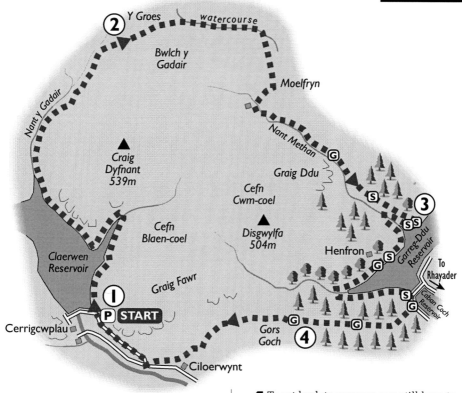

dropping into the bottom, and pass through a gate into woodlands, through which a delightful path will convey you down to the side of Garreg Ddu Reservoir.

3 *The shores of Garreg Ddu provide a profound contrast to those of Claerwen. Deciduous woodland envelops this side of the reservoir, and in springtime wild flowers carpet the ground.* Turn right. At first the path is narrow, but very clear (indeed, waymarked), and it works its way around the small inlet of the Methan, through fields, over stiles and past the remnants of some defunct pre-flooding estate walls. *These are the walls to the grounds of the vanished house of Cwm Elan, where the poet Shelley stayed in 1811 and 1812.* Further along the shore of the reservoir, the path joins a more definite track, which takes you around another inlet and out to the road at the chapel.

4 To get back to your car you still have to go back over the hills you have already traversed. The return journey is, however, direct and straightforward. Pass the church and go through the gate on the left immediately beyond it. Follow the track, steeply uphill and alongside a stream, all the way through the forest, going straight across the crossroads in the middle. After some exertion you will reach a gate that opens out onto the moorland of Rhos y Gelynnen. Follow this track all the way across the moor, *enjoying the views of Drygarn Fawr's plateau and crowning cairns.* After passing a telecommunications mast, until recently one of only a few man made structures standing on the Elenydd, the track leaves the forest boundary behind and heads off down into the valley beyond. Before it arrives at Ciloerwynt house, a right hand branch (signposted, but initially unclear on the ground) will take you down onto the road. A slightly cruel, but mercifully short, climb up tarmac will take you back to your car.

WALK 16

Y GAMRIW

DESCRIPTION A varied walk which combines hillwalking in open country up to 2,000 feet in altitude with wandering along wooded lanes. Eleven miles in length, involving some fairly steep ascents, it will take a good five and a half hours.

START Car park near Dolymynach Reservoir.

DIRECTIONS Leave Rhayader on the B4518. Pass Elan village and travel along the side of Caban Coch Reservoir. Take the left turn, over a causeway, and follow the road left below the chapel. Just beyond the end of the reservoir system there is a small car park tucked into the hillside on the right hand side. **The upland sections of this walk need to be treated with respect during inclement winter weather.**

I Cross the bridge over the Claerwen directly in front of the car park and continue past Llanerch Cawr Farm, keeping left along the track which skirts the south of Dolymynach Reservoir. Once the southern tip of the reservoir is rounded, and soon after fording a small stream (Nant Ddu), the track splits into a high route and a low route. Take the high route which heads up and across the side of the swell of ground called Moelfryn, heading for the corner of the forestry plantation ahead.

2 The track runs along the boundary of the forest, gradually climbing around the broad western spur of Gro Hill. Follow it all the way up the forest boundary, contour around the cwm of Nant y Glo and head up to the ruins of Ty'n y Pant. From the ruined house bear round to the right and continue to follow the track up to the bwlch above, which is scattered with ancient cairns, and head directly downwards initially on a rough track, and then on a metalled road between hedges, into the valley bottom.

3 Turn right at the junction in the valley bottom and follow the road for about two miles. *Ambling along the road is a delight-*

ful experience, and the easy going allows efficient expenditure of energy in anticipation of the climbing yet to come. Sessile oak woodland alternates with scrubby meadows, with the flanks of Y Gamriw providing a dramatic and anticipatory backdrop. Eventually, just after the road leaves the trees behind, and immediately opposite the entrance to Crownant Farm, a bridleway leaves the road on the right hand side.

Caban-coch Reservoir

Dolymynach Reservoir

Dam

START

P

Llannerch Fawr

4 Take this right exit, which gives access to the north ridge of Y Gamriw. An immediate obstacle is a ford, which if crossed directly will result in wet feet. Fortunately it can be avoided by the use of the footbridge just downstream. Cross the field and follow the obvious track diagonally up the hillside. After negotiating a couple of rickety gates, the track continues to cross the hillside obliquely, clinging to the uppermost field boundaries. After half a mile, there are opportunities to zig-zag up the hillside. Do so, and gain the ridge of Y Gamriw. The going is steep here and there, but the vegetation is for the most part cropped and steady underfoot. A series of cairns confirm correct progress, and the ridge becomes more shapely as height is gained, its steep southern slopes creating a fine airy atmosphere.

32

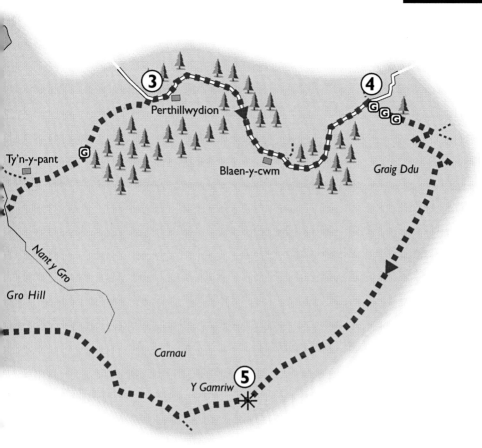

Ty'n-y-pant · G

Perthillwydion

Blaen-y-cwm

Graig Ddu

Nant y Gro

Gro Hill

Carnau

Y Gamriw **5**

5 After less than two miles of upward progress, the summit of Y Gamriw is won. *It boasts a good selection of cairns, a trig point and a curious ruin. The point gives particularly fine views of the Radnor Forest to the east. To the south lie the Black Mountains and unfolding westwards are the flat heights of the Cwmdeuddwr hills.* To return to your car traverse the summit of Y Gamriw and bear off right along an indistinct path. Follow this, initially keeping the head of an obvious valley on your left, then crossing a shallow bwlch to descend more definitely around the southern fringe of Gro Hill. By keeping the gentle detached elevation of Gro Hill to your right, you will arrive back at the forest boundary which was followed earlier in the day. Turn left, and retrace your earlier steps back to the car.

Caban-coch

DRYGARN FAWR

DESCRIPTION A demanding hill walk to the highest point of the Elenydd. The going can be quite wet and tussocky, and the route crosses a largely featureless plateau. **Care needs to be taken in low visibility, or in winter when shelter can be very hard to find.** On a clear day the huge horizons include Pumlumon, The Radnor Forest and all the mountains of South Wales. Allow at least four and a half hours for the eight and a half miles.

START Car Park near Dolymynach Reservoir.

DIRECTIONS Leave Rhayader on the B4518. Pass Elan village and travel along the side of Caban Coch Reservoir. Take the left turn, over a causeway, and follow the road left below the chapel. Just beyond the end of the reservoir system there is a small car park tucked into the hillside on the right hand side.

I Take the road directly opposite the car park, and cross the bridge over the Afon Claerwen. Head briefly towards the farmhouse of Llanerch Cawr at what appears to be the end of the track, but double back right, through a gate, before you get there, and follow a minor road *which is flanked by an interesting stone fence of a type common in Radnorshire.* Take the first track on the left which quickly gives access to the valley of the Rhiwnant. From this point on the walk takes on an air of wildness. A land rover track runs alongside the Rhiwnant, and then begins to climb away into the neighbouring Cwm Paradwys. The Rhiwnant falls away below, hemmed in by its craggy valley, and awaits our re-acquaintance later in the walk.

2 Ignore the right turn, and follow the track until it begins to double back up the hillside. At this point a thin path may be traced winding its way through the tussocks above the eastern bank of Nant Paradwys. After winding uphill for a little over a mile the track arrives at Bwlch Y Ddau Faen, the

dip which separates Drygarn Fawr from its easterly neighbour, Gorllwyn. Careful attention to the ground will reveal another path through the tussocks which strikes off in a westerly direction. Take this. The price of missing it is a belated detour through ankle deep tussock grass back to the main drag, although a trip to the cairns at Carnau is a worthwhile addition to the walk.

3 The track heads up onto Drygarn's plateau, and then winds through sometimes boggy land towards the summit. At first the outcrop on Carreg yr Ast makes its presence felt, but it is quickly marginalised as the summit cairns of Drygarn Fawr come into view. Head along the now more obvious track directly for the great cairns, which stand at the apex of the Elenydd.

4 *The summit of Drygarn Fawr is a curious hump. The few metres it protrudes from the surrounding moorland are just enough to make it the defining feature of the plateau. Ancient man emphasised this by adding a pair of huge cairns, which have in a more recent century been lovingly rebuilt. The larger of the two, which marks Drygarn's highest point, is a good eight feet in height and perfectly constructed. This, the most remote of the 2,000 foot summits in Wales, is a place to linger for as long as you can. Pumlumon dominates the northern perspective. The long scarp of the Black Mountains, the Brecon Beacons and the westerly Black Mountain draws the eye across the southern horizon beyond the militarised Mynydd Epynt. Wind turbines intrude to the north and north-east, and the fringes of the Tywi forest creep upon the western horizon, but no other significant*

Rhiwnant

Creigiau Hir

(4)

Drygarn Fawr

reminders of the last century enter the scene – as yet. If plans for the huge wind power project to the west, at Camddwr, go ahead, Drygarn Fawr will be hemmed in by up to 200 turbines. For now, though, the open perspectives of the Elenydd, its colours constantly shifting with the light and the seasons, allow the eye and the senses full freedom of manoeuvre. Once you have taken your fill

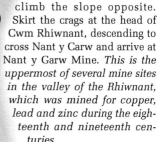

START

P

G **1**

Mine

5

Rhiwnant

Craig yr Dalrhiw

Dalrhiw

Nant Paradwys

Waun

Carreg yr Ast

2 climb the slope opposite. Skirt the crags at the head of Cwm Rhiwnant, descending to cross Nant y Carw and arrive at Nant y Garw Mine. *This is the uppermost of several mine sites in the valley of the Rhiwnant, which was mined for copper, lead and zinc during the eighteenth and nineteenth centuries.*

5 From the mine a track leads all the way down Cwm Rhiwnant. After the heavy going of the upper Rhiwnant, this will be a delight. Fast progress combines with commanding views of the craggy, wild valley below, and will **3** restore any spirits lost in the tussocks. The track eventually leads to a ford across the Rhiwnant, which will guarantee

of Drygarn's summit, head directly north across the open country for less than a mile and descend into the hollow of Pant Glas. This is tough going in places, but eventually you will hit the infant Rhiwnant. Follow this downstream. The going continues to be rough, and care is needed in places. In wet weather the tributaries running into the Rhiwnant will require a positive approach. The best strategy, although the least inviting initially, is to cross the Rhiwnant and

wet feet, if by some miracle you haven't already got them. If you don't fancy this, or there has been very heavy rain, you will need to escape back to the tarmac using the system of tracks and bridleways which bear off to the left further downstream. Otherwise, after the ford the track climbs up and rejoins the route into Cwm Paradwys, allowing you to retrace your first steps of the day back to your car.

LLYN CARW

DESCRIPTION An upland walk to a remote mountain lake with variable going under foot. A less challenging hillwalk than Drygarn Fawr, with many (but not all) of Drygarn's qualities. The route is just over seven and a half miles (depending upon how directly you tackle the tussocks!), and up to four hours should be allowed. Expect to get wet feet!

START Parking Place near Dolymynach Reservoir.

DIRECTIONS Leave Rhayader on the B4518. Pass Elan village and travel along the side of Caban Coch Reservoir. Take the left turn, over a causeway, and follow the road left below the chapel. Just beyond the end of the reservoir system there is a small car park tucked into the hillside on the right hand side.

I Cross the bridge over the Claerwen, and bear right, away from the farm of Llanerch Cawr, as in **Walk 17**, but shortly after entering Cwm Rhiwnant take a turn on the right, which drops down and fords the river. Wet feet are unavoidable on this trip, and you will do well to avoid them at this juncture! Once across the river, the track passes a small stand of conifers which shelters a ruined habitation. Shortly afterwards a right branch begins to climb the hillside in earnest. This is an old miners' track, embanked and clinging to the hillside in places and indistinct in others, which eventually reaches Nant y Garw Mine at the top of the valley. Follow it all the way to the mine.

2 Pass through the ruins of the mine and continue, steadily climbing, along the banks of Nant y Carw. This stream will take you up into the heart of the Elenydd. The going gets progressively rougher underfoot as you progress upstream and tussock grass begins to dominate the vegetation. Turn off, and follow the second tributary which enters the Carw from the left after about a mile. The source of this small stream is Llyn Carw, and another ten minutes of toil up through the

boggy tussocks will bring you to its shores. *Llyn Carw is one of the smaller natural lakes of the Elenydd, and lies serenely in a hollow beneath the gentle ridge of Cerrig Llwyd y*

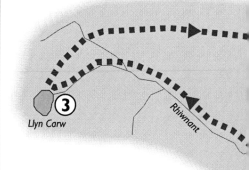

Llyn Carw

Rhestr. The views from its reedy banks are not spectacular, although Drygarn Fawr makes its presence felt emphatically enough to the south east. The attraction of the place is more in the feeling of isolation and loneliness which permeates, and the sharp contrast to the surrounding moor provided by Carw's small sheet of water and surrounding brilliant green rushes. This is an ideal place to unpack the rucksack, take off the boots and recline for an hour or so on a warm summer's day.

3 Having meditated upon Drygarn's summit across Carw's cloud reflecting waters for long enough, the homeward journey may begin. A bridleway skirts the northern banks of the lake which ultimately leads south into the Irfon Valley. Ignore the temptation to follow this further into the wilderness, and head north along it toward Pen Maen-wern. After crossing a small stream, the track bears to the east away from the summit of Pen Maen-wern. *It is, however, worth departing from the track briefly to visit the standing stone at Pen Y Maen. This impressive quartz icon provokes wonder at its long past ritual function.* Having admired the stone, cut back south onto the distinct track and follow it across the moorland, from which it ultimately descends steeply back to Rhiwnant. A maze of tracks wander the hill above

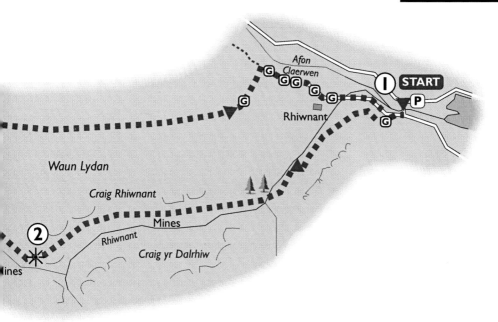

Rhiwnant, and all lead down to the farm. The best route is to climb out of the hollow lane, which forms the bridleway, onto the nearby rough track which descends through gates and bears right into the valley bottom past Rhiwnant farm. After the farm continue along the metalled road back to the car.

Drygan Fawr

THE MONK'S TROD

DESCRIPTION A linear walk along an ancient green road which was once part of a route connecting the Cistercian abbeys of Strata Florida in Ceredigion and Abbey Cwm Hir in Radnorshire. This route is one of the highlights of any walking itinerary in Mid-Wales, and provides a relatively easy traverse of the wild and empty interior of the Elenydd. The return journey to the outcrop above Llynoedd Cerrigllwydion is approximately nine miles, and will occupy four hours of gentle wandering.

START Pont ar Elan.

DIRECTIONS From Rhayader head south along the B4518, but instead of going to Elan village, take the right turn at Cwmdeuddwr signposted as the mountain road to Aberystwyth. Follow this until a left turn, signposted to Elan Village, heads down to the bridge over the Elan. There is a small car park just over the bridge.

hillside along the line of least resistance. *The first thing that will strike you about the route is the damage done by the despicable activities of off-road motor-bikers and drivers. When I first walked this route, some twenty years ago, much of it was in perfect condition underfoot. The medieval routeway was, for much of its length, a simple hollow in the moorland. Unfortunately, the activities of irresponsible off-roaders have now reduced sections of it to a quagmire. Natural erosion has bitten into the ruts scored by mechanised wheels and turned them into deep channels, which are particularly noticeable on the first ascending section. This amounts to the vandalism of an ancient monument, and it is, alas, still going on. As the track has become more unusable, the vandals have made diversions and spread the damage onto the surrounding moor. Do not be put off by this, and controlling your anger at the perpetrators, con-*

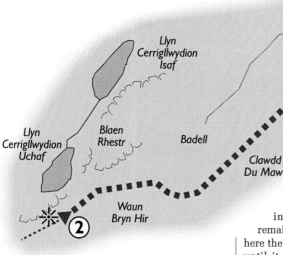

tinue your climb around the head of Cwm Torclawdd. At a little less than two miles from the road the track crests the ridge of Clawdd Du Bach, passing the rather denuded and forlorn remains of the cairn of Carn Ricet. From here the Monks' Trod follows the broad ridge until it reaches its highest point above the beautiful Llyn Cerrigllwydion Uchaf, amidst lonely rock outcrops. *This spot is one of the most delectable in all Wales, and the atmosphere is timeless. Using the outcrops as a vantage point you may admire the two lakes*

I From Pont ar Elan follow the minor road which heads down to Craig Goch Dam for a little under half a mile until it is possible to join the Monk's Trod, which climbs the

of Cerrigllwydion, beautifully set in the rock strewn emerald greenness below. In the other direction Drygarn Fawr's presence belies its distance across the intervening Claerwen Valley. All around the Elenydd laps like a sea. The Monk's Trod continues around the 'great hollow' of Pant Mawr and descends to ford the Claerwen at Rhyd Hengae. *Walkers with access to two cars, or those prepared to stay overnight at Pontrhydfendigaid, have the option of following the trod across the Claerwen, past the sublime Teifi Pools and*

to Pont ar Elan is a delight to walk, despite the patches of damage to the track. The only intrusions are the legions of turbines to the North East, and the thought that more are on their way. Fortunately, the turbines drop out of view as the Trod descends and the final motif of the walk is the view across the Craig Goch Dam below on the right. *To*

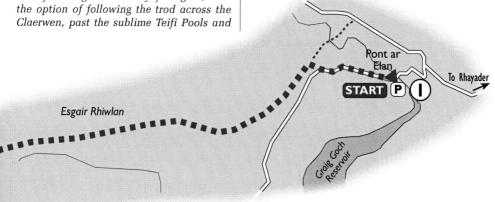

down to Strata Florida. The full traverse makes a classic day's walk, but those without the time or transport will need to retrace their steps back to Pont Elan.

2 The journey back is, however, no anticlimax. The attractions of seeing the views backwards compensate for having to leave the whole traverse for another day. The gentle gradient from Carn Ricet down

the informed walker, even this will provoke thought. Looking to the future, there are plans for a massive expansion of the Elan Valley system which will dramatically raise the water level and flood even more of the Elan Valley's beauties. With thoughts like these burning through the tranquillity which is offered by the walks in this book, you will descend the Monk's Trod resolving to make the most of this special area now.

Craig Goch Reservoir from
the Monk's Trod

GWYN LLYN

DESCRIPTION A gentle walk around a charming lake which lies cradled in the arms of the uplands to the east of Rhayader. Just under five miles in distance, but easy going. Allow two hours.

START Rhayader Town Centre. Parking outside Rhayader can reduce the distance.

the route begins to change. The road begins to rise up above the valley revealing the picturesque lake of Gwyn Llyn below. *An extensive patch of sessile oak clothes the steep mossy boulder-strewn slopes on the right; a fragment of what would have once been a far more extensive woodland cloak.*

2 An obvious track soon drops away from the road into the valley bottom on the left. Ignore the unwelcoming PRIVATE sign (there is a public footpath) and follow the track down through woodland into the flat valley bottom. Continue, ignoring a minor detour to the left, to a stream crossing at the head of the valley. From here a path winds indistinctly up the hillside, quickly to join a more distinct bridleway. Turn left along this bridleway and follow it around the foot of the hill.

3 Finally contouring around the toe of the uplands, *with views of Gwynllyn ever-present on the left*, the track will quickly

Glanllyn

Treheslog Farm G Gwynllyn

Rhayader **START**

A470

B4518

I *At the centre of Rhayader is the town clock, which was erected as a memorial for those who gave their lives in the Great War.* From here head along the main shopping street of the town with the Spar shop on the left. Cross the bridge over the Wye and head out of town along the B4518. You will soon enter the adjoining village of Cwmdeuddwr, which gives its name to the range of hills unfolding across the Wye Valley to the south. Take the right hand turn signposted as the mountain road to Aberystwyth. Stroll along the unclassified road, passing some mature deciduous woods on the left, as it begins to climb the side of the valley. After about a mile the character of

bring you to the rather intimidating gates of Treheslog Farm. Pass directly through the farm and take the obvious track on the left. This climbs gently until it reaches an unclassified metalled road. Bear to the left at the junction and follow the road as it gradually descends to the Rhayader/Aberystwyth mountain road. Turn left back into Cwmdeuddwr, and thence back to Rhayader.